What's Cooking?

by Mary Solins

Harcourt

Orlando Boston Dallas Chicago San Diego

Visit *The Learning Site!*
www.harcourtschool.com

Do you like to help cook? Here are some good things to make. Just follow the directions.

Wash and peel some carrots
and potatoes. Peel some onions,
too. Cut them into pieces.

Put the vegetables in a pot on the stove. Add some meat and a cup of very hot water. Add salt and pepper, too.

What's cooking?
Stew!

Put two cups of flour in a
mixing bowl. Stir in two
teaspoons of baking powder.
Add a bit of salt, too.

Add six tablespoons of butter.
Use a fork to mix the butter
into the flour. Then add a cup
of milk and stir.

Use a spoon to drop the batter
onto greased cookie sheets.
Bake them in the oven at 450
degrees.

What's cooking?
Biscuits!

Choose some fresh, juicy
vegetables. Wash some lettuce.
Tear it into pieces.
Put the lettuce in a big bowl.

Cut the vegetables into small
pieces. Put them in the bowl,
too. Add some oil and some
vinegar.

What are we making?
Salad!

Wash and peel some apples.
Cut them into pieces.

Put the apple pieces in a pot.
Put the pot on the stove.
Add some cinnamon and sugar.

What's cooking?
Applesauce!

Everything is ready. Let's sit down to eat. What do we have? Dinner!